Contents

 Ireland		4
Land		6
Landmarks		8
Homes		10
Food		12
Clothes		14
Work		16
Transport		18
Language		20
School		22
Free time		24
Celebrations		26
The Arts		28
Factfile		30
Glossary		31
Index		32

Ireland

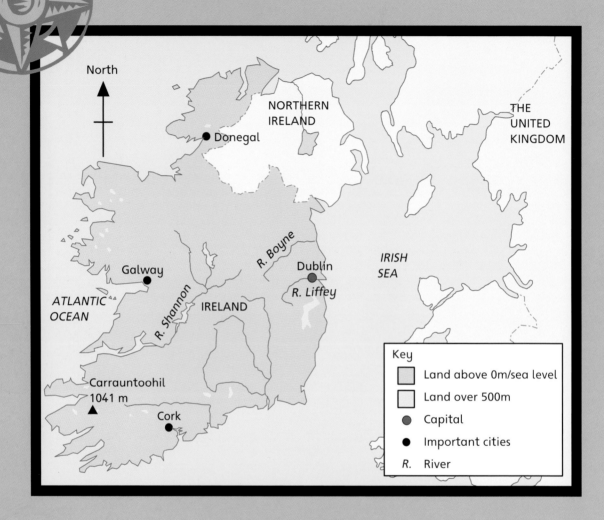

North

NORTHERN
IRELAND

● Donegal

THE
UNITED
KINGDOM

R. Boyne

Galway ●

Dublin ●
R. Liffey

IRISH
SEA

ATLANTIC
OCEAN

R. Shannon

IRELAND

Carrauntoohil
1041 m
▲

Cork ●

Key

Land above 0m/sea level

Land over 500m

● Capital

● Important cities

R. River

Ireland is in northern **Europe**.
The north-east corner of the island
is called Northern Ireland and it is
part of the United Kingdom.

Ireland has lots of land. Most people
live spread out over the country. About
one and a half million people live in
or around Dublin, the **capital**.

Land

The centre of Ireland is low, flat farmland and **bog**. There are mountains around the coast. These beautiful, rounded mountains are not very high.

The land looks green all year round because it has so much rain. Winds bring clouds from the Atlantic Ocean. These drop rain as soon as they reach Ireland.

Landmarks

There are many **ancient** graves around Ireland. The most famous one is at Newgrange. It is over 4000 years old. Sunlight only reaches inside it on 21 December.

The Burren is in the west of Ireland. It is a huge, windswept area of rock with underground caves. There is nowhere else like it in all of **Europe**.

Homes

There are still a few **traditional** cottages. These are built from stone and have just one room. They have **thatched** roofs and a plot of land for growing food.

About 150 years ago, cruel landowners
forced most people to move off their land
to towns or overseas. Today many people
live in modern houses in towns.

Irish people usually eat their main meal at lunchtime. It might be Dublin coddle, a stew of sausages, bacon, onions and potatoes.

Traditionally, Ireland makes a lot of different breads and potato dishes, and the **dairies** make very good cheeses. There is also lots of fresh seafood.

Clothes

Ireland is famous for its **textiles**. Sheep provide wool which is woven into beautiful clothes. You can still buy handmade Aran jumpers from Galway, or beautiful **tweed** from Donegal.

In the last few years, some top **fashion designers** have moved to Dublin. Business is good for new designers and shops.

Work

Many farms are still small and people grow just enough food for themselves. In the west, there are beef and **dairy** farms. **Crops** grow better in the east, where it is not so wet.

Many people work in factories, making food or drink, like Guinness, the famous Irish beer. Glass, computers, metals, chemicals and **textiles** are also made.

Transport

It is easy to travel to and from other parts of **Europe** by both sea and air. Ireland has three **international** airports, and its own airline, Aer Lingus.

Almost all travel within Ireland is by road. There is also the Dart, a train route on part of the east coast.

Language

English and Irish are the two **official** languages of Ireland. The Irish language was brought to Ireland about 2000 years ago by people from Eastern **Europe**.

Everyone learns Irish at school, and road signs are written in English and Irish. Some people in the west of Ireland still speak Irish as their main language.

School

Children go to primary school between the ages of six and twelve. The day starts at nine in the morning and finishes at about three in the afternoon.

Students have to go to secondary school from the age of 12 to 15. Their days are longer and they have more homework.

Free time

Many Irish people enjoy watching or playing sport. Race meetings attract huge crowds and many young people keep their own ponies, even in the cities!

On Sunday, some families watch their local teams play **traditional** games. Hurling is a fast game played with a stick and ball. In **Gaelic** football, the players are allowed to hold the ball.

Celebrations

The Irish Derby at Kildare is held in June. It is an important day for many Irish people and horses from all around the world take part in the race.

A special day for every **Catholic** child is their First **Communion**. Everyone goes to church in their best clothes. Each child chooses a saint's name to add to their own.

The Arts

Long ago, each Irish village had its own storyteller. Some of their stories were written down in beautiful books. Ireland has produced many famous writers.

Almost every village has a **traditional** music group. People play the fiddle, the tin whistle, the uileann pipes and the bodhrán (a small goatskin drum). They play dance tunes and old **Gaelic** songs.

29

Factfile

Name The full name of Ireland is the Republic of Ireland.

Capital The **capital** city is Dublin.

Language **Gaelic** Irish and English are the two **official** languages of Ireland.

Population There are about three and a half million people living in Ireland.

Money The Irish have the Irish pound or punt (IR£) which is divided into 100 pence.

Religion Almost all Irish people are **Catholics**. About three out of 100 people are **Protestant**.

Products Ireland produces wheat, barley, potatoes, milk, **livestock**, beer, machinery and transport equipment.

Words you can learn

aon (ayn)	one
dó (doe)	two
trí (three)	three
tá (thaw)	yes
níl (knee)	no
dia dhuit (dee-a-gwit)	hello
slán agat (slawn-aguth)	goodbye
le do thoil (le-do-hull)	please

Glossary

ancient	from a long time ago
bog	land that is always wet and spongy
capital	the city where the government is based
Catholic	Christians who have the Pope in Rome as the head of their Church
Communion	the Christian ceremony of eating bread and wine
crops	the plants that farmers grow and harvest (gather)
dairies/dairy	the type of farm that produces milk, cheese and yoghurt
Europe	the collection of countries north of the Mediterranean Sea
fashion designers	people who draw ideas for, and make, clothes
Gaelic	the **ancient** language of the people who first lived in Ireland, Wales and Breton, or describing anything that belonged to them
international	to do with countries all around the World, not just Ireland
livestock	animals kept on a farm for their meat or milk
official	decided by the government
Protestant	Christians who do not have the Pope as the head of their Church
textiles	cloths or fabrics
thatched	roofs made from thick layers of straw or reeds
traditional	the way things have been done or made for a long time
tweed	a thick, woven, wool fabric

Index

Catholic   27, 30, 31

Dublin   4, 5, 12, 15, 30

Europe   4, 9, 20, 31

factories   17

First Communion   27, 31

Gaelic   25, 29, 30, 31

Gaelic games   25

horse racing   24, 26

Irish Derby   26

mountains   5, 6

music   29

Protestant   30, 31

textiles   14, 17, 31

First published in Great Britain by Heinemann Library,
Halley Court, Jordan Hill, Oxford OX2 8EJ,
a division of Reed Educational and Professional Publishing Ltd.

Heinemann is a registered trademark of Reed Educational & Professional Publishing Limited.

OXFORD   MELBOURNE   AUCKLAND
JOHANNESBURG   BLANTYRE   GABORONE
IBADAN   PORTSMOUTH (NH) USA   CHICAGO

Designed by AMR
Illustrations by Art Construction
Printed and bound in Hong Kong/China by South China Printing Co.
03 02 01 00
10 9 8 7 6 5 4 3 2 1

ISBN 0 431 08346 0

This title is also available in a hardback library edition (ISBN 0 431 08341 X).

British Library Cataloguing in Publication Data

Bell, Rachael
  A visit to Ireland
  1. Ireland – Juvenile literature
  I.Title II.Ireland
  941.5

Acknowledgements
The Publishers would like to thank the following for permission to reproduce photographs:
Brian Kelly p 23; Collections: Michael Diggin p 6, George Wright pp 10, 13, Michael St Maursheil pp 14, 20, 25; Hutchison Library: P. Moszynski p 21; Images Colour Library: pp 7, 26; Image Ireland: Alain Le Garsmeur pp 8, 19, Geray Sweeney p 18; J. Allan Cash Ltd: pp 9, 16; Photo Images Ltd: pp 11, 24, 27; Rex Features London: Steve Wood p 15; Robert Harding Picture Library: Duncan Maxwell p 17; The Bridgeman Art Library: Board of Trinity College Dublin p 28; Tony Stone Worldwide: Oliver Benn p 5; The Slide File: pp 12, 22, 29.

Cover photograph reproduced with permission of Tony Stone Images/John Fortunato.

Every effort has been made to contact copyright holders of any material reproduced in this book. Any omissions will be rectified in subsequent printings if notice is given to the Publisher.

Any words appearing in bold, **like this**, are explained in the Glossary.

A Visit to
IRELAND

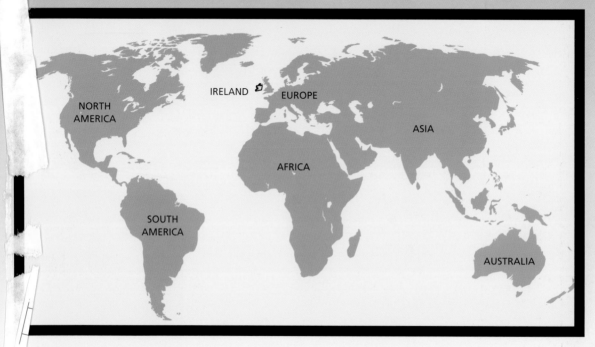

IRELAND

EUROPE

NORTH
AMERICA

ASIA

AFRICA

SOUTH
AMERICA

AUSTRALIA

Rachael Bell

Heinemann